The Cat Lover's
Book of Days

by Mimi Vang Olsen

WITH TEXT BY RONNIE LEONARDS

1817

HARPER & ROW, PUBLISHERS, New York

Cambridge, Philadelphia, San Francisco, London
Mexico City, São Paulo, Sydney

FIRST EDITION

Designed by Lydia Link

ISBN: 0-06-015040-8

82 83 84 85 86 10 9 8 7 6 5 4 3 2 1

The Cat Lover's Book of Days

1

New Year's Day
He stalks in beauty like the night.

2

Catliness is next to Godliness.

3

A kitten saved is a kitten blessed.

4

The fog comes
on little cat feet.   —CARL SANDBURG, "Fog"

5

Who knows what mischief lurks in the hearts of cats? You do.

6

But thousands die, without or this or that,
Die, and endow a college, or a cat.
—ALEXANDER POPE, *Moral Essays, III*

7

Here's to laughter and the love of cats!

8

"All was dark as a stack of black cats in a coal cellar."
—JOHN S. ROBB

9	10
Yes, cats dream.	A cat wager: Heads I win, tails you lose.

11

One good cat deserves another.

12

Save a stray. Spay!

13

"Because" is a cat's reason.

14

Hippolyte Taine decreed the wisdom of cats was infinitely superior to the wisdom of philosophers.

15

An ID tag on a safe collar is a must for the cat who may roam from home.

16

Cats make great alarm clocks!

17

In certain parts of England it's believed that if a cat turns its tail toward the fire, it will snow; if it licks its tail, it will rain.

18

"Our perfect companions never have fewer than four feet." —COLETTE

19

It's so nice to have a cat around the house.
It's even nicer to have two.

20

"As easy as a cat could lick her ear." —SEBA SMITH

21

The cat in gloves catches no mice. —ENGLISH PROVERB

22

A cat is a cat is a cat.

23

Feline philosophy: You scratch my back and
I won't scratch yours.

24

I've got a little cat,
And I'm very fond of that. —JOSEPH TABRAR

Mimi Vang Olsen

25

There's no accounting for taste! Ask any cat.

26

Do I love you, dear pussycat?
You bet your puss 'n' boots I do!

27

The cat would eate fish, and would not wet her feete.
—JOHN HEYWOOD, *Proverbs*

28

Vanity, thy name is cat.

29

An ideal time to separate a kitten from its mother
is at eight weeks.

30

He bought a crooked cat, which caught a crooked mouse.
—MOTHER GOOSE

31

In ancient Japan, cats accompanied the fishermen on their
voyages to ensure safety and success.

1

The cat has nine senses: Touch, taste, temperature, sight, smell, hearing, balance, direction, and time.

2

A hiss may be worse than a bite. Maybe.

3

"She watches him, as a cat would watch a mouse."
—JONATHAN SWIFT

4

Home is where your cat is.

5

In ancient Egypt, the male cat represented the moon,
the female the sun.
Night and Day, you are the one. . . .

6

A cat to everybody is a cat to nobody.

7

There are about twelve million stray cats in the U.S.
Save a homeless cat.

8

A harmless necessary cat.
—WILLIAM SHAKESPEARE, *The Merchant of Venice*

Mimi Vang Olsen

9

10

Love me—love my cat.

Leftover vegetables? Good. Mix them into Tabby's food!

11

Catnip: It's love at first bite.

12

Curiosity killed the cat; satisfaction brought him back.
—ENGLISH PROVERB

13

I never met a cat I didn't like.

14

Happy Valentine's Day!
Love covers a multitude of cats.

15

Hell hath no fury like a hungry cat!

16

Cat tip: A wet brush works wonders when grooming your cat.
The hair won't fly!

17

18

The more you stroke a cat, the more it lifts its tail. —PROVERB

A cat may look on a king. —JOHN HEYWOOD, *Proverbs*

19

You can fool some cats some of the time, but
you can't fool any cat all of the time.

20

Pussy cat, pussy cat, where have you been?   —MOTHER GOOSE

21

In 1950, the London *Times* reported that a four-month-old kitten
scaled the Matterhorn with a group of mountaineers.

22

Promise her anything, but give her a cat.

23

"Charm us, orator, till the lion look no larger than the cat."
—ALFRED, LORD TENNYSON

24

Cats love to hear well of themselves.

Mimi Vang Olsen

25

26

"Talking as soft and as mealymouthed as could be, like an old gray cat, mewing round a bird cage." —ANN S. STEPHENS

The cat is hungry when a crust of bread contents her. —PROVERB

27

A cat of beauty is a joy forever.

28

The *Katzenjammer Kids* (cats) have appeared in newspaper comics all over the world for over seventy-five years!

1

2

A house is not a home unless a cat lives there.

"But buds will be roses and kittens, cats."   —LOUISA MAY ALCOTT

3

"Puss" is derived from Pasht, the Egyptian Moon Goddess.

4

Here's to the cat! Long may it live, live, live, live, live, live, live, live, live.

5

Cats run in where angels fear to tread.

6

Somewhere, someplace, a cat is waiting in a cage. Adopt.

7

The cat does not catch mice for God.   —PROVERB

8

Cat tip: Clip Kitty's claws when he's sleepy.
It's less wear and tear!

9

10

In a cat's eyes all things belong to cats.   —ENGLISH PROVERB

I had rather be a kitten and cry mew,
Than one of these same metre ballad-mongers.
   —WILLIAM SHAKESPEARE, *Henry IV, Part I*

11

Sweet mews is good mews.

12

Plain yogurt is a useful substitute for milk.

13

Never leave a drawer open with a cat around!

14

"One of the most striking differences between a cat and a lie is that a cat has only nine lives." —MARK TWAIN, *Pudd'nhead Wilson*

15

Ah sweet mystery of life, at last I've found you, pussycat.

16

A cat who is loved is on good footing with the world.

17

St. Patrick's Day

I named my kitten Ol' Blue Eyes,
The bluest eyes I've ever seen.
As he began to learn his name,
Ol' Blue Eyes' eyes turned green!

18

Speak low when you speak love to your cat.

19

Everthing comes to the cat who waits . . .

20

What was that lump I saw under your sheet last night?
That was no lump, that was my cat!

21

A man is known by the cat he keeps.

22

The cat on your hearthstone to this day presages,
By solemnly sneezing, the coming of rain!   —ARTHUR GUITERMAN

23

A cat with little ones never has a good mouthful.
—FRENCH PROVERB

24

Many blue-eyed white cats are born deaf. They compensate with
sharp vision and a keen sense of smell.

Mimi Vang Olsen

25

26

The gingham dog went "Bow-wow-wow!"
And the calico cat replied "Mee-ow!" —EUGENE FIELD, "The Duel"

" . . . someone to love and someone to love you, a cat, a dog, and a pipe or two." —JEROME KLAPKA JEROME, *Three Men in a Boat*

27

Cats give a purpose to the elderly and the lonely.

28

Advice to a fat cat: Don't cry over skimmed milk.

29

It's said that President Wilson read *Krazy Kat* each morning during breakfast.

30

"Cats, like men, are flatterers." —WALTER SAVAGE LANDOR

31

Cat kin: Someone who can relate to a cat.

Mimi Vang Olsen

1

April Fool's Day
A fool and his cat are soon parted! Use an ID tag.

2

And who can practice the art of meditation better than the cat?

3

The ideal of calm exists in a sitting cat.
—JULES RENARD

4

A spay in time saves nine.

5

Some very arduous couples mate ten times in an hour!

6

Cat tip: Make no bones about it. No bones for Tabby!

7

Now that you have a cat, have you learned the art of going to bed?

8

Dumb, inscrutable and grand,
So Tiberius might have sat,
Had Tiberius been a cat.   —MATTHEW ARNOLD, "Poor Matthias"

9

10

"O sweet are the slumbers of the virtuous cat."   —JOSEPH ADDISON

Oh, that reassuring pounce on the bed,
Every time I rest my head . . .

11

Has your cat had her dental checkup lately?

12

The cat did it!

13

To cats all things are possible.

14

It is said that the Prophet Mohammed cut off his sleeve upon arising to avoid disturbing his sleeping cat.

15

"The cat is never vulgar." —CARL VAN VECHTEN

16

The first American cat show was held at Madison Square Garden in 1895.

Minni Vang Glenn

17

18

My Love She Is a Kitten
And My Heart's a Ball of String.
—HENRY SAMBROOKE LEIGH, "My Love and My Heart"

Must be true about the cat's pajamas.

19

A kiss or a hiss, it all depends on you.

20

Cats are the best bed warmers.

21

It's better to be alone with your cat than in boring company.

22

While rain depends, the pensive cat gives o'er
Her frolics, and pursues her tail no more. —Jonathan Swift

23

Cats are stubborn things

24

Cat chat: An alleycat? I'm an American Domestic Shorthair, please!

Mimi Vang Olsen

25

26

The sound of music is the can opener.

"You must step as slow, and silent and cautious as a cat."
—IRVING WOLFERT

27

Nothing is impossible to a determined cat.

28

Chortle, chortle, pussy cat
How I wonder where you're at.

29

Maou. That's "cat" in Egyptian. Mao. That's "cat" in Chinese.

30

Whoever cares well for cats will marry happily.
—FRENCH PROVERB

1

Truth is like a cat and always comes down on its feet.
—EARLY AMERICAN PROVERB

2

Have you cuddled your cat today?

3

If man could be crossed with the cat it would improve man, but it would deteriorate the cat. —MARK TWAIN, *Notebook*

4

Cat tip: A screen in every window!
    Cats sometimes lose their footing.

5

Try stretching out with a newspaper while the cat's around!

6

The more you love and play with your kitten, the more it will love and play as a cat.

7

Caroline's Tom Kitten resided in the White House during the Kennedy Administration.

8

"There are no ordinary cats." —COLETTE

9

Contortionist, thy name is cat.

10

When your cat presents you with a mouse, it's a sign of affection!

11

Don't try changing a typewriter ribbon with a cat around.

12

"A smile for all the world as sweet as a cat makes at a new pan of milk."   —THOMAS CHANDLER HALIBURTON

13

A black cat in Britain means good luck!

14

Who is to bell the cat? It is easy to propose impossible remedies.
                —AESOP

15

None of us liveth to himself . . . but the cat.

16

Expectant mother: A catful o' miracles.

Mimi Vang Olsen

17

18

Let the cat out of the bag and she'll jump right back in again.

Sure way to get your cat to come out of hiding:
Open the refrigerator.

19

To each his own cat.

20

But the kitten, how she starts,
Crouches, stretches, paws and darts!
—WILLIAM WORDSWORTH, "The Kitten and the Falling-Leaves"

21

Morris (the first) was living on borrowed time:
He was adopted from a Humane Society branch in
Hinsdale, Illinois, in 1968. The rest is history.

22

Though my cat is absent in body, she is still present in spirit.

23

Never try to thread a needle with a cat around.

24

Wild cat strike: A swat in the head, to oust you from bed!

Mimi Vang Olsen

25

26

The sign of the cat is everywhere!

The love of cats is the root of all kindness.

27

A queen may mate with many males in one evening.
Oh, mad and marvelous night!

28

A woman hath nine lives like a cat.   —OLD ENGLISH PROVERB

29

Cat got your tongue? Then keep quiet!

30

Cat Fancy, organized in England in 1887, is now known as
the National Cat Club.

31

The cat is by nature a political animal.

JUNE

Mimi Vang Olsen

1	**2**
Who can decorate a window as beautifully as a cat?	A nuzzle under kitty's chin is sure to make him grin.

3

Reflections:
Mirror, mirror, on the wall, who is fairest of us all?
You, pussycat!

4

A frame to a painting as a window to a cat.

5

Feline philosophy: What's yours is mine . . .

6

The Owl and the Pussy-Cat went to sea
In a beautiful pea-green boat.   —EDWARD LEAR, *Nonsense Songs*

7

Bringing home another cat? Ask a friend to enter with it.
It's less traumatic.

8

In ancient Egypt, anyone who harmed a cat was punished by death!

9

10

A little cat told me . . .

"There is, indeed, no single quality of the cat that man
could not emulate to his advantage." —CARL VAN VECHTEN

11

Don't try to make the bed when the cat's around.

12

Guy de Maupassant couldn't write unless a cat was present.

13

Alleycat or aristocat is still a pussycat.

14

Try saying no to a cat!

15

"A kitten is more amusing than half the people one is obliged to live with."   —Lady Sylvia Morgan

16

An orphaned kitten depends upon the milk of human kindness.

Mimi Vang Olsen

17

Cats fit into everything. Everything!

18

The cat will out!

19

To look like the cat that swallowed the canary —Yiddish proverb

20

To know a cat is to love a cat.

21

Like water off a cat's back!
As he grooms, he waterproofs his coat.

22

"The smallest feline is a masterpiece."   —Leonardo da Vinci

23

Dick Whittington and his cat really existed!

24

Kit-Chin: Located below the whiskers and above the neck.

25

26

Kitty lib: If there is dogma—why not catma?

When your cat kneads you, consider it a compliment.

27

The cat in the manger.

28

How we love to be loved by our cats, and what we do to be loved!

29

Such doggerel—such catterel!

30

. . . on the catwatch shift . . .

JULY

Mimi Vang Olsen

1

Dignity, thy name is cat.

2

When a mouse laughs at a cat there is a hole nearby.
—NIGERIAN PROVERB

3

_____
_____
_____

Cat walk: Door-top edges   Bathtub ledges
            Garden hedges   Secret wedges

4

_____
_____
_____

Independence Day
"I love cats because I love my home, and little by little they become
   its visible soul."
                                        —JEAN COCTEAU

5

_____
_____
_____

All cats are kittens at heart.

6

_____
_____
_____

"Wild as a kitten she was, but as harmless too."   —ANN S. STEPHENS

7

_____
_____
_____

Who says beggars can't be choosers? No cat I know!

8

_____
_____
_____

Pope Leo XIII treasured Micetto, a Vatican-born kitten, and carried
him around in the folds of his robes.

9

Cat's cradle: A hat box, a shoe box, any old box.

10

If a cat is vain, flatter. If shy, flatter . . .

11

My cat gives me a klutz complex.

12

A cat's stairway to paradise is a ladder.

13

To have a cat is to be its master . . . and its slave.

14

A happy cat walks with its tail high up in the air.
Not a worry, not a care.

15

How about a tail, Miss Manx? "No thanx."

16

Cats can see in the dark, it's true,
But in total darkness they have no point of view!

Mimi Vang Olsen

17

18

There's more to a meow than meets the ear.

"It has been the providence of nature to give this creature nine lives instead of one."
—PILPAY

19

It was the purr of the moment . . .

20

"But I never heard of [a cat] who suffered from insomnia."
—Joseph Wood Krutch, *The Twelve Seasons*

21

Let the female cat run; the tomcat will catch her.
—German proverb

22

Cat tip: Fish must be served boneless, cooked, and fed sparingly!

23

A calm person . . . a calm cat.

24

Wherever there's the faintest glimmer of sun, your cat is sure to find it.

25

A cat is an "all natural" mousetrap.

26

"The cat is the companion of the fireside." —EDWARD E. WHITING

27

The cat is the original sun worshipper.

28

"If you are worthy of its affection, a cat will be your friend but never your slave."
—Théophile Gautier

29

Teach me to do thy will. You can bet no cat ever said that!

30

Through the ages, around the world, farmers believed cats ensured good harvests.

31

"I tawt I taw a putty cat."   —Tweetie Bird

©Mimi Vang Olsen

1

Art imitates cats.

2

Cats are emotional blackmailers!

3

Between you, me, and the scratch post . . .

4

Felix the Cat of the silent movies was in such popular demand that by 1923 he had his own comic strip in the newspapers.

5

Cats affectionately rub noses,
Just like Eskimoses.

6

Kittens are curious. You know what they say about curiosity . . .

7

It is more blessed to adopt a cat in need
Than to carelessly breed.

8

Cats are "all natural" fly swatters.

9

10

Manipulator, thy name is cat.

The cat makes sure whose chin it may lick.   —PROVERB

11

Cats know how to pull strings. Even the wrong ones!

12

"When I play with my cat, who knows whether I do not make her more sport than she makes me?" —MICHEL DE MONTAIGNE, *Essays*

13

All the times I scold you when you are only being a cat, I must remember that . . .

14

A cat is an automatic dishwasher.

15

Cats shed under stress.

16

"Ah! cats are a mysterious kind of folk. There is more passing in their minds than we are aware of . . . " —SIR WALTER SCOTT

17

Some of my best cats are friends.

18

The Chinese believed you could tell the time of day by looking into the eyes of a cat.

19

A snort of catnip is a safe and "legal" high.
Give some to your kitty and watch her fly!

20

Why waste good leftovers? Supplement canned food with fresh food.

21

Einstein loved cats.

22

How often have you noticed that just before a storm breaks, your cat becomes tense and nervous?

23

The cat is the original nonconformist.

24

Exotic? Neurotic? Quixotic? Hypnotic? Psychotic? Erotic?
Your cat or you?

Mimi Vang Olsen

25

To please himself only, a cat purrs.   —Proverb

26

"Cats know how to obtain food without labor, shelter without confinement, and love without penalties."   —W. L. George

27

What's virtue in man can't be vice in a cat.
—MARY ABIGAIL DODGE, *Both Sides*

28

Every "pure black" cat has at least one white hair . . . somewhere!

29

Any woman who is referred to as catty . . .

30

"The Cat's Fugue," a piano piece by Domenico Scarlatti, was inspired by a kitten on the keys.

31

As perfectly pink as a pussycat's nose.

SEPTEMBER

Mimi Vang Olsen

1

2

Tell me about your cat and I'll tell you about mine!

A cat is a lion in a jungle of small bushes. —PROVERB

3

Cat tip: Try a little cottage cheese.
It's tasty, and high in calcium.

4

The first English book on cat care, by Lady Cust, was published in 1856.

5

The cat is a law unto itself.

6

The Chinese believed the wink of a cat's eye signified the coming of rain.

7

A paper bag's a price-less toy.
It provides your cat with endless joy.

8

Cats make you laugh at yourself.

9

10

Many well-cared-for cats have lived to twenty and over!

A cat has a mind of its own.

11

Remarked a Tortoise to a Cat:
Your speed's a thing to marvel at . . .
—AMBROSE BIERCE, "The Vain Cat"

12

No workman can build a door which shall be proof against
a cat or a lover.   —FRENCH PROVERB

13

A Buddhist belief says that the dark cat brings gold, the
light cat brings silver, and all cats bring good luck.

14

Your every mew is my command.

15

Familiarity breeds unwanted kittens.

16

Rumor has it our American Domestic Shorthairs arrived here on the
Mayflower in 1620.

Mimi Vang Olsen

17

18

And who can outstare a cat?

A little fresh green grass is beneficial for the digestion and for getting rid of furballs.

19

An occasional sweet for kitty is a treat.
Like chicken soup, it couldn't hurt.

20

Some cats are truly royal! They go on and on, with just one Tom, and that my friend is loyal!

21

"Quick as a kitten playing with dead leaves."
—Henry David Thoreau

22

The Nekomatabashi Bridge in Tokyo is dedicated to a heroic cat.

23

Cat tip: With a kitten around, keep the toilet lid down!

24

You can't teach an old cat new tricks. Sometimes you can't teach a young cat new tricks.

25

Yet must I humble me thy grace to gain—
For wiles may win thee, but no arts enslave.
—Graham R. Tomson, "The Fireside Sphinx"

26

The first cat show took place at the Crystal Palace in London, 1871.

27

I like little Pussy, her coat is so warm;
And if I don't hurt her she'll do me no harm.
—JANE TAYLOR, *Rhymes for the Nursery*

28

"No matter how much cats fight, there always seem to be
plenty of kittens."
—ABRAHAM LINCOLN

29

My precious cat, my one and only,
   Come play with me, I'm lonely.

30

The Isle of Man issued a coin in 1970, with Queen Elizabeth on one
side, the Manx cat on the other.

Mimi Vang Olsen

1

2

To love is human, to purr is divine.

"Speechless as cats in cloudy weather . . ." —WILLIAM PYNCHON

3

High diddle diddle
The cat and the fiddle . . .   —MOTHER GOOSE

4

A cat has a sense of humor when not at its own expense.

5

An old cat knows fresh milk.   —PROVERB

6

In ancient Egypt, upon the death of the family cat, the members of the household would shave their eyebrows as a sign of mourning.

7

A cat after my own heart.

8

Cardinal Richelieu had fourteen cats, and left them a small fortune in his will.

9

10

If cat lovers wore crowns, we'd all be royalty.

The Cat's Protection League in Slough, England, was founded in 1927, and was devoted exclusively to the welfare of cats.

11

A dogwood tree . . . why not a catwood?

12

The cat that has its mouth burned by drinking hot milk will not drink even buttermilk without blowing upon it.
—Indian proverb

13

"Ez soshubble ez a baskit er kittens."
—Joel Chandler Harris, *Uncle Remus and His Friends*

14

A mother and her kittens, accidentally trapped in a packing case, survived a six-week journey from Detroit to Egypt!

15

Set thine house in order. With a cat around?

16

To get your attention a cat will do anything, anything!

Mimi Vang Olsen

17

18

Rejoice with me. I have found the cat!

Sing, sing! What shall I sing?
The cat's run away with the pudding string.   —NURSERY RHYME

19

The first Rex was discovered in 1950, on a farm in Cornwall, England.

20

O libidinous cat, you leave behind with each encounter something of yourself.

21

Don't try using a tape measure with a cat around.

22

Inside every fat cat a thin one is trying to get out. Don't overfeed!

23

A cat is excellent social security.

24

Pet was never mourned as you,
Purrer of the spotless hue,
Plumy tail, and wistful gaze
While you humored our queer ways.
   —THOMAS HARDY, "Last Words to a Dumb Friend"

Mimi Vang Olsen

25

Lose yourself . . . with your cat.

26

A prance, a dance, a swat for fun
And that is known as hit and run!

27

Lord Chesterfield left a pension for his cat.

28

"A cat which is kept as a household pet may properly be considered a thing of value. It ministers to the pleasure of its owner."
It's a law!

29

Every cat has its day.

30

Every black cat is not a witch. —FRENCH PROVERB

31

Halloween

A new broom sweeps clean, if you can shake off the cat.

Mimi Vang Olsen

1

It is better to feed one cat than many mice.
—NORWEGIAN PROVERB

2

The Scots believe that tortoiseshell cats bring good health to the home.

3

Lips that touch mousies shall never touch mine.
Well, hardly ever.

4

Every cat has its own reason for being.

5

The eternal sex symbol. The cat.

6

If a girl treads on a cat's tail, she will not find a husband before
the year is out.   —FRENCH PROVERB

7

"Would you like cats if you were me?" replied the
mouse.—LEWIS CARROLL, *Alice's Adventures in Wonderland*

8

The Egyptians considered the cat a semidivine creature with
worldly powers.

9

A living sculpture. A cat.

10

Stately, kindly, lordly friend
Condescend.
—ALGERNON CHARLES SWINBURNE, "To a Cat"

11

A cat doesn't care anything about reason,
he just knows what he likes.

12

When the cat's away . . . catch up on your sewing.

13

"The cat has too much spirit to have no heart."
—Ernest Menault

14

My cat gives me a sense of balance.

15

It's so much fun to watch a cat pounce
And break into that "side step" bounce!

16

There is no scientific explanation for the cat's purr.

° Mimi Vang Olsen

17

Having a cat is its own reward.

18

A lame cat is better than a swift horse when rats infest the palace. —PROVERB

19

Puss came dancing out of a barn
With a pair of bagpipes under her arm.   —NURSERY RHYME

20

I never knew I was a servant until I had a cat.

21

As many cats, so many minds, every cat his own way.

22

"As full of fun as a kitten."   —THOMAS CHANDLER HALIBURTON

23

Winston Churchill's cat sat in on wartime cabinet meetings.

24

Six little mice sat down to spin:
Pussy passed by and she peeped in.   —MOTHER GOOSE

Mimi Vang Olsen

25

26

If a person has a cat, the cat "has" the person.

Cat tip: When clipping Kitty's claws, clip only the tip.
If you see pink, avoid it!

27

The cat shuts its eyes while it steals cream.
—Early American proverb

28

Have you played with your cat today?

29

"You should be as silent as cats in a kitchen."   —John P. Kennedy

30

Minnaloushe creeps through the grass
Alone, important and wise,
And lifts to the changing moon
His changing eyes.
—William Butler Yeats, "The Cat and the Moon"

Mimi Vang Olsen

1

To bell the cat is to save the birds.

2

Dame Trot and her cat
Sat down for a chat
The Dame sat on this side
And puss sat on that. —Nursery rhyme

3

_____

_____

Have cats. It's a second existence.

4

_____

_____

Neutering helps to prevent straying and spraying.

5

_____

_____

My cat could have me in his pocket . . . if he had one.

6

_____

_____

My cat is a white-collar worker. He pushes pencils.

7

_____

_____

When a cat's around, never leave a letter in the typewriter.

8

_____

_____

Cats of all shades are masters of fun.

9

Stroke your cat with words.

10

"When all candles be out, all cats be gray." —JOHN HEYWOOD

11

To find a kitty . . . is serendipity.

12

Never put the kit to watch your chickens.   —PROVERB

13

You want to sleep . . . Cat wants to play
Guess who gets whose way!

14

The Manx has a funny habit. It hops like a bunny rabbit.

15

Cats make fools of us all. Who cares?

16

If the cat growls, beware!

Mimi Vang Olsen

17

Don't try to wrap a package unless the cat's asleep.

18

"When I have a convenient reason, I will call for you," said the cat.

19

"He was as docile as a kitten." —MARGARET JUDD

20

Talmudic lore forbids anyone to enter a darkened house that does not contain a cat.

21

If there's dog-Latin, why not cat-Latin?

22

I have no treasures but my cats.

23

The devil found plenty of mischief for idle cats to do!

24

Christmas Eve

And visions of Ping-Pong balls bounced in their heads.

Mimi Vang Olsen

25

Christmas Day
Merry Christmas, Pussycat!

26

Cats know something we don't know. Probably many things.

27

Never, ever, try to start a jigsaw puzzle when the cat's around!

28

"Tell me," said Alice . . . "why your cat grins like that?"
"It's a Cheshire cat," said the Duchess, "and that's why."
—LEWIS CARROLL, *Alice's Adventures in Wonderland*

29

"As meek as a gray cat with a dab of cream on her whiskers."
—ANN S. STEPHENS

30

I'm cat tired!

31

New Year's Eve
And that's Cat.

Notes

Notes

Notes

Notes